THE MESSAGE OF *AMORIS LAETITIA*

THE MESSAGE OF *AMORIS LAETITIA*

FINDING COMMON GROUND

WALTER KASPER

TRANSLATED BY WILLIAM MADGES

Paulist Press
New York / Mahwah, NJ

Cover image by Apostrophe/Shutterstock.com
Cover and book design by Lynn Else

Originally published in 2018 by Verlag Herder as *Die Botschaft von Amoris laetitia: Ein freundlicher Disput*

Library of Congress Cataloging-in-Publication Data
Names: Kasper, Walter, 1933– author.
Title: The message of Amoris laetitia : finding common ground / Walter Kasper ; translated by William Madges.
Other titles: Botschaft von Amoris laetitia. English
Description: New York : Paulist Press, 2019.
Identifiers: LCCN 2019005033 (print) | LCCN 2019980153 (ebook) | ISBN 9780809154289 (pbk. : alk. paper) | ISBN 9781587688225 (ebook)
Subjects: LCSH: Catholic Church. Pope (2013– : Francis). Amoris laetitia. | Families—Religious aspects—Catholic Church. | Marriage—Religious aspects—Catholic Church. | Love—Religious aspects—Catholic Church.
Classification: LCC BX2351.C2963 K3713 2019 (print) | LCC BX2351.C2963 (ebook) | DDC 261.8/358—dc23
LC record available at https://lccn.loc.gov/2019005033
LC ebook record available at https://lccn.loc.gov/2019980153

ISBN 978-0-8091-5428-9 (paperback)
ISBN 978-1-58768-822-5 (e-book)

Published by Paulist Press
997 Macarthur Boulevard
Mahwah, New Jersey 07430
www.paulistpress.com

Printed and bound in the
United States of America

CONTENTS

CONTENTS

PREFACE

My lecture before the Consistory of Cardinals on February 20 and 21, 2014, "The Gospel of the Family," which was published under the same title (Paulist Press, 2014), unleashed a lively discussion. Unfortunately, it focused exclusively on the last chapter, concerning the question of possibly admitting the divorced and remarried to the sacraments.

The apostolic exhortation *Amoris laetitia* (2016), based on the gospel and the discussions from both episcopal synods of 2014 and 2015, led to a broader and more profound understanding of the many current and pressing issues concerning marriage and family. The great majority of the people of God have enthusiastically welcomed this exhortation as a liberating and good message about experiencing joy in family life. The exhortation, unfortunately narrowed down to one single point, has become the object of severe contention by some people.

Avoiding every kind of polemic, I would like to try to show that *Amoris laetitia* does not represent new teaching, but presents, based on the gospel, a creative renewal of the tradition and completely corresponds to the renewed view of the Second Vatican Council concerning marriage and family. It is also in accord with the teaching of the two previous pontificates while simultaneously advancing them in a careful way.

Of course, there can be—and there must be—different schools of opinion in a Church that calls itself Catholic. Consequently, we do not need to be anxious about discussions. We should conduct them in such a way that they serve unity and prove to be a service to joy in love. That alone is the concern of this small volume, written in friendly solidarity with all who are of a different opinion.

Cardinal Walter Kasper
Advent 2017

INTRODUCTION

Hardly has any other apostolic exhortation been so eagerly anticipated and hardly has any other in recent Church history elicited such a heated discussion since its appearance as *Amoris laetita*, "The Joy of Love" (2016). The exhortation was anticipated because questions about marriage and the family belong to the most pressing questions of the present age. The family, which is *the* primordial institution of humanity, especially in the Western world, has fallen into a crisis. Marriage and family are the cradle of humanity; marriage and family concern no less a matter than the future of humanity and especially the future of Europe.

Renewal must derive from the cradle of humanity and the cradle of every single human being. That is also true for the Church. Pope John Paul II and Pope Benedict XVI have, therefore, declared, "The family is the way of the Church."[1] Pope Francis moves along the same line as both of his predecessors: "The joy of love experienced by families is also the joy of the Church" (*Amoris laetitia* 1).[2] The Church grows, lives, suffers, and experiences joy with families; in families and through them, the Church is present in the midst of life and in the midst of the world.

In light of this dramatic situation, it appears grotesque that the internal Church discussion concerning *Amoris laetitia* has become bogged down in the eighth chapter, in fact, bogged down with regard to one single note in the eighth chapter, and really with only one single sentence there (*AL* 305, note 351). In this sentence, the issue is whether people in so-called irregular situations, including remarried divorced individuals, can be allowed to receive communion in certain cases. Without a doubt, that is *a* pressing pastoral question, but it is not *the* question, nor is it *the* topic of *Amoris laetitia*. *Amoris laetitia* is in the first place not about what the Church can do in so-called irregular situations; rather, it is about how the Church can be of help in avoiding such situations, wherever possible. The exhortation wants to show what and how the Church can contribute positively to achieving the joy of love in marriage and the family (*AL* 307). The Church especially wants to assist young people in finding the happiness of their lives and discovering joy in love, which the great majority even today seek in matrimonial partnership and in the family.

The cardinal mistake of many contributions to the discussion is that they treat the internal ecclesial and internal theological question, which has become the bone of contention, in isolation from the basic intention and the total context of the apostolic exhortation. In the process, they ignore the prophetic vision of the text, which—as it will be shown—stands entirely in the tradition of the Church and advances it in a consistent way.[3] On account of this constriction, the discussion becomes like a discussion between willfully deaf people, who speak next to each other but not really with each other. If, conversely, one places the issue in dispute within the total context, then it becomes an interesting, paradigmatic problem, whose resolution can turn out to be pioneering with regard to many other pressing issues. The presupposition for the success and fruitfulness of such a dialogue is, of course, that one first immerses him- or herself in the vision of *Amoris laetitia* in general and allows him- or herself to be challenged by it.

NOTES

1. Pope John Paul II, Letter to Families, February 2, 1994; Pope Benedict XVI, Address on the Thirtieth Anniversary of the Publication of the Apostolic Exhortation *Familiaris consortio*, December 1, 2011.

2. Hereafter cited as *AL*.

3. The discussion was lately shaped above all by the *Dubia*, which four cardinals initially submitted to the pope and then made public. Because of the open letter of a great number of laypeople and theologians offering fraternal correction of the pope on account of spreading or permitting heresies, an intolerable situation has been evoked, about which one cannot remain silent. None of the seven implicated sentences is contained in *Amoris laetitia* or in any other document of the pope. At root, it has to do with misrepresentations that no theologian I know holds. In the meantime, one of the best experts concerning the philosophy and theology of Pope John Paul II, Rocco Buttiglione, has published *Riposte amichevoli ai critici di Amoris laetitia*, with an extensive, introductory essay by Cardinal Gerhard Ludwig Müller (Milan: Ares, 2017). This publication has shown that the feared and sometimes alleged contradictions between Pope John Paul II and Pope Francis do not exist. Thus, the *Dubia* of the four cardinals in the matter are answered. Moreover, in the just-mentioned book, it is clear that there are substantial opportunities for agreement between the different positions. Even if they have not yet led to complete unanimity, nonetheless they have come to the conviction that, regarding the still-remaining different positions, we are dealing with different schools of thought that rest on the common foundation of the Church's teaching. Of course, there can be and should be further discussions about these differences. The accusation of heresy, however, has no place in this discussion. Except for the magisterium, who, then, has the right publicly to raise such an accusation? Is the principle no longer valid that everyone is to be considered ecclesially orthodox, as long as he or she was not legitimately condemned?

ABBREVIATIONS

AA *Apostolicam Actuositatem.* Second Vatican Council, Decree on the Apostolate of the Laity (1965).

AL *Amoris laetitia.* Pope Francis, Apostolic Exhortation on Love in the Family (2016).

DH Heinrich Denzinger, Peter Hünermann et al., *Compendium of Creeds, Definitions, and Declarations on Matters of Faith and Morals* (San Francisco: Ignatius Press, 2012).

DV *Dei verbum.* Second Vatican Council, Dogmatic Constitution on Divine Revelation (1965).

EG *Evangelii Gaudium* (Joy of the Gospel). Pope Francis, Apostolic Exhortation on the Proclamation of the Gospel in Today's World (2013).

FC *Familiaris consortio.* Pope John Paul II, Apostolic Exhortation on the Role of the Family in the Modern World (1981).

GS *Gaudium et spes.* Second Vatican Council, Pastoral Constitution on the Church in the Modern World (1965).

LG *Lumen gentium.* Second Vatican Council, Dogmatic Constitution on the Church (1964).

UR *Unitatis redintegratio*, Second Vatican Council, Decree on Ecumenism (1964).

Chapter 1

COMPANIONSHIP FOR THE JOURNEY BY A CHURCH ON THE WAY

The great significance that the Church and Pope Francis attribute to the family arises solely from the fact that *Amoris laetitia* was prepared during not one but two episcopal synods, the extraordinary synod of 2014 and the ordinary synod of 2015. This already uncommon preparatory process was again preceded by another uncommon process: for the first time before a synod, there was a worldwide survey of the faithful.

A SURVEY THAT PACKS A PUNCH

Behind the long preparation and survey of the faithful, there lies the conviction that the magisterium of bishops and the pope must first be a "listening office" before it is a teaching office. Without a doubt, it must listen to the Word of God, which is attested to in Holy Scripture and in Scripture's interpretation in the tradition of the Church. The tradition consists not only of magisterial documents, which normally are scarcely accessible to the great majority of the faithful, and then only with difficulty. It is constituted above all in the liturgy, which at least practicing Christians celebrate every Sunday and on the major feast days, and it is communicated in the people of God's sense of the faith (*sensus fidelium*). Every Christian has a share in the sense of faith as a result of his or her baptism.

The Second Vatican Council did not hesitate to say, "The entire body of the faithful, anointed as they are by the Holy One (see 1 John 2:20, 27), cannot err in matters of belief" (*LG* 12).[1] Pope Francis adds, "The same Spirit who inspired the Gospels and who acts in the Church also inspires the preacher to hear the faith of God's people and to find the right way to preach at each Eucharist" (*EG* 139).

The survey, as it was conducted before the synod, is, of course, not the testimony of the entire body of the faithful; it is, however, an indication worth noting of the sense of faith of the faithful. A bishop and pastor must—in the words of Martin Luther—listen to what the people say. That is especially true when we are dealing with marriage and the family. For in that case, not celibate clerics but the fathers and mothers of families are the first experts; they are the ones who have the experience (*experientia*) and, therefore, are the ones who must be heard first of all.

These observations do not supersede the special responsibility and authority granted by Jesus Christ, such as the special charism of the magisterium. These observations also do not turn it into a kind of highest notary, which only has to confirm what is factually present in the Church as its consciousness of faith. The magisterium has the right to bind and to loose (Matt 16:19; 18:18). Nevertheless, the distinction that was often previously made between the teaching and the listening Church is obsolete. All who are in the Church have to listen to the Word of God and to one another, and they have to bear active witness to the faith. The special teaching and pastoral office that belongs to the bishops, especially to the Bishop of Rome, has its own special place within the community of the faithful.

Thus, the results of the surveys were, in fact, not binding, but nonetheless they merited attention. What we came to hear from these surveys was also informative. First, we heard that the desire, especially of young Christians, for a happy married and family life is, now as before, unbroken. The surveys made it clear that marriage and family are not some kind of discontinued model. On the contrary, even today they are the life-project and happiness-project of most people (*AL* 1). The Church's message concerning marriage and family, therefore, is responding to a deep human desire. Precisely in a time in which many other institutions are in crisis and so many things have become uncertain, marriage and family are for many the place that provides a home, where they seek to experience human happiness and fulfillment.

Admittedly, a second result provides the occasion for critical reflection. In the survey, it became clear that a chasm exists between the Church's teaching on marriage and family and the lived faith conviction of a large number of Christians. Many Christians can no longer comprehend many aspects of the Church's moral teaching concerning sex, marriage, and family.

Those who had some pastoral experience were not surprised by this finding. Some others, however, had first to gasp a little for air while reading the results of the survey.

THE WAY OF FINDING CONSENSUS THROUGH THE SYNOD

What is to be done? Right at the beginning of the synod, the pope made clear that he wanted an open discussion; he wanted *Parhesia*. *Parhesia* is an important biblical word, which means something like candor. The invitation to *Parhesia* led during the synod to an open and sometimes also contentious debate such as I had not experienced at earlier synods in which I could participate. This new, fresh tone did good because without frank debates, one cannot solve problems. In his opening statement, the pope, of course, quickly added that humility must be combined with candor, that is, the readiness to listen to what others likewise are candidly saying.

For such a frank and simultaneously humble listening to one another, it may be helpful to remember the rule that Ignatius of Loyola proposes right at the beginning of his Exercises: Every good Christian must be more eager to put a good interpretation on a neighbor's statement (i.e., understanding it in the sense of right faith) than to condemn it. If one, however, is not able to interpret it favorably, then he or she looks into how the other understands it, and if that meaning is bad, then he or she should correct the other with love. If that is not sufficient, he or she should search out all appropriate means so that the statement may be saved by understanding it properly.

The pope himself was the most attentive listener. At the

conclusion, he said that all of us had left the synod different from how we had entered it; we had learned from each other. Thus, at the end, there was sizable agreement concerning the issues that had been put to a vote, including a two-thirds majority when concerning each of the critical questions. The long discussions and the contentious arguments, therefore, paid off.

In his post-synodal exhortation *Amoris laetitia*, the pope abided by the result of this vote; he did not go beyond it, but he also did not stay even one millimeter behind it. Many sections of the exhortation are virtually a mosaic of statements from the synods. Therefore, whoever now criticizes *Amoris laetitia*, that person not only criticizes the pope but also puts him- or herself in opposition to the majority opinion of the entire episcopate that was represented in the synod. Both of these things are unusual and also unheard of in the Catholic Church. An apostolic exhortation of the pope, after consultation of the faithful and of the bishops, is, according to Catholic teaching—so say the First as well as the Second Vatican Councils—a binding statement of the ordinary magisterium of the Church (see DH 3011; *LG* 25).[2] Everyone is free to express his or her opinion in an appropriate form. However, it cannot be the case that individuals now declare themselves to be a self-appointed super-magisterium.

Amoris laetitia is the result of a process of consensus building in the Church, and it puts into effect what one today means by synodality.[3] The Greek word *synodos* translated literally means "together on the way." Communal ways of building consensus were already the way of the apostles' council in Jerusalem (Acts 15; Gal 2) as well as the way of the great general councils of the ancient Church, which formulated the basis of the common confession of all Eastern as well as Western churches to this very day. They too were the result of an often-difficult struggle, which then continued in a spirited fashion after the respective council, similar to the situation today after the Second Vatican Council. After the council's definition, in each case it became a matter of reception, expressed somewhat simplistically: it was a question of the interpretative sovereignty of the previous council.

When similar processes unfold today, that is in itself no reason for anxiety or particular commotion. Even today there is no alternative to the way of listening to one another and discussing with one another. Only by means of candid and simultaneously humble communication (*communicatio*) in joint listening to the Word of God, which is binding for all, can the Church take concrete shape as a community (*communio*) in one faith. Every Christian is invited to take part in this candid and simultaneously humble communication, corresponding to his or her knowledge, experience, and responsibility in the Church.

AN UNDERSTANDING OF LIVING TRADITION

The way of finding consensus through synods is not the path of accommodation to the situation. The Church cannot simply regurgitate what *people* today say, what *people* today think, and what *people* today are doing. "Do not be conformed to this world," says the Apostle Paul (Rom 12:2). Therefore, *Amoris laetitia*, right in the second section, clearly distinguishes itself from those who, so to speak, want to upset the apple cart and turn things on their head (*AL* 2). The Holy Spirit is not at work today for the first time; he was also at work in the past.

Therefore, we may not be so arrogant to opine that today for the first time in the Church the light has gone on, while in the past nearly everything was dark and went wrong.

Alongside the synchronic dialogue, that is, the dialogue between the different positions in the contemporary Church, we must also seek the diachronic dialogue, that is, the dialogue between earlier positions and new beginnings today. As the pilgrim people of God, the Church is the same in every century. The Church, however, is not some dead skeleton, but rather a living organism that is animated by God's Spirit. There cannot be a novel innovation in the Church, but certainly the Church must travel the path of continuous renewal (see *LG* 8; *UR* 4). The Second Vatican Council says, through the Holy Spirit, God is constantly in conversation with the Church, the bride of his son. Therefore, in the Holy Spirit there can be no improvement in revelation, but indeed there can be progress in understanding the truth that has been revealed once for all (see *DV* 8).[4]

Pope Benedict has also given clear expression to this point. In his well-known first address to the members of the Roman Curia concerning the interpretation of the Second Vatican Council, he opposed a hermeneutic (interpretation) of discontinuity, as if the Second Vatican Council had broken with the preconciliar Church and had begun a new Church. To the hermeneutic of discontinuity, however, he did not counterpose an unhistorical rigid interpretation but rather a hermeneutic of reform, that is, a conjunction of fidelity and dynamism, the interaction of continuity and discontinuity.[5] Briefly stated: There is no new postconciliar Church; however, the council wanted to make, over against some preceding appearances of advanced age and torpor, a Church that was becoming rejuvenated and renewed today, just as Pope John XXIII expressed it with his vision of an aggiornamento.

Both synods of bishops have also gone on this path of renewal through synchronic and diachronic consensus building; it is also the path of *Amoris laetitia*. From this it follows that one must interpret the teaching of *Amoris laetitia* in the light of the tradition, but that one must also understand the tradition in the light of new spiritual insights. That was the path that all councils, especially the Second Vatican Council, have taken. To express this point pictorially: The tradition is not standing water, which becomes vapid and putrid with the passage of time. Through the Holy Spirit working in it, the tradition is a continually fresh, bubbling spring. In this sense, *Amoris laetitia* says right at the beginning that it cannot refrain from enlarging upon some doctrinal, moral, spiritual, and pastoral questions (*AL* 2). In fact, simply to repeat one more time what has already been said would have been boring. For that, there would have been no need for the effort of two synods.

NOTES

1. The teaching concerning the sense of faith (to be distinguished from the faith consensus of all the faithful) was, on the basis of Holy Scripture and the tradition of the Church fathers, developed in the nineteenth century, above all by Johann Adam Möhler, Josef Matthias Scheeben, and John Henry Newman. The Second Vatican Council took up this teaching. In the process, it also took a considerable step toward an important concern of the Reformation. If one takes this teaching seriously, it requires a reconsideration of the understanding and praxis of the Church's teaching office. With that said, after more than fifty years after the council, we are standing only at the beginning. The International Theological Commission has extensively discussed these issues and recorded the result of this discussion in the document *Sensus fidei in the Life of the Church* (2014). Pope Francis has addressed the issue multiple times in his programmatic first apostolic exhortation, *Evangelii gaudium* (nos. 119, 139, 198).

2. According to this teaching, the statements of the ordinary magisterium (encyclicals, apostolic exhortations, among others) are to be accepted with religious submission of will and understanding (*LG* 25). They are not to be considered infallible, unless they would explicitly raise this claim for individual propositions. That is not the case with *Amoris laetitia* or with the respective earlier encyclicals and apostolic exhortations. All of them formally have the same authority. Therefore, it is inappropriate when some now try to bring earlier doctrinal statements into opposition to *Amoris laetitia*. It is normal that there are different emphases and even further developments between these documents, which were composed in part in different situations. It was not in the least different regarding the councils of the first few centuries. However, there can be no talk of a break or of contradictions, as should be demonstrated in what follows.

3. Concerning this, see the address of Pope Francis during the synod on the family on October 17, 2015, on the occasion of the fiftieth anniversary of the creation of the bishops' synod. The pope

thereby succeeded well in showing that synodality and primacy do not exclude each other but, on the contrary, mutually complement each other.

4. This understanding of a living tradition is likewise developed based on patristic theology in the nineteenth century by Johann Adam Möhler and John Henry Newman and then is taken up by Vatican II. Accordingly, tradition is not only a body of content, which is passed from hand to hand like a defunct coin, but is the process of actively handing on, in which each new generation or different culture receives in the Holy Spirit that which has been handed on as permanently valid and simultaneously actively understood. Finally, the process of transmission is the self-transmission of the exalted Lord in the Holy Spirit to abiding presence in the Church. This process is never terminated and frozen, as it were, either with a council or with a certain pontificate. Jesus has promised that the Holy Spirit will lead us into all truth until the end of the world (John 16:13). In this sense, a further phase in the reception of the council and of the reception of the preceding pontificates has begun with the present papacy in order to pass on to the future, with creative fidelity, what has been transmitted.

5. See Benedict XVI, Speech to the Members of the Roman Curia, December 22, 2005. Pope Benedict apparently was guided by John Henry Newman, who has shown that this kind of development is more than a purely logical explication. See *An Essay on the Development of Christian Doctrine* (New York: Appleton, 1845; New York: Cambridge University Press, 2010).

Chapter 2

MARRIAGE AND FAMILY AS A JOURNEY, MARRIAGE PASTORAL CARE AS ACCOMPANIMENT ON THE WAY

By describing the Church as a community of the way, we have picked up a foundational word from Holy Scripture. It describes the way of God with Abraham and the patriarchs, the way of the Old Testament people of God through the desert. Jesus Christ has walked the way with his disciples. As with the way to Emmaus, this way led through difficult and often oppressive questions and crises. Only at the end did the eyes of both disciples on the road to Emmaus open (Luke 24:13–35). The Acts of the Apostles describes Christianity as the new way

(Acts 19:9, 23; 24:22). According to John's Gospel, Jesus Christ is the way, the truth, and the life (John 14:6).

MARRIAGE AND FAMILY AS A JOURNEY

For Pope Francis, marriage and family are also a journey. Again and again in *Amoris laetitia*, there is talk of the journey and of the story of love (*AL* 9); in like manner, there is talk of the path of life (*AL* 19–22), of the partners as companions on life's path (*AL* 163), of the growth and maturation of love (*AL* 133–35, 221), of the learning process in marriage and family (*AL* 136). Even after the wedding—thus says *Amoris laetitia*—marriage is not a finished product (*AL* 211, 218) but a continuing task (*AL* 232). The bonds of wedlock—according to *Amoris laetitia*—must be joined anew again and again (*AL* 164).

This metaphor of the journey, which is used by Pope Francis, is not merely an appealing, rhetorical cliché; rather, something very fundamental is expressed by it, something that is essential for the overall understanding of *Amoris laetitia*. With this metaphor, the pope differentiates his position from a cold armchair morality (*AL* 312), which seeks to solve everything by means of undue deductions from abstract theological principles (*AL* 2). He does not want to be guided by an abstract idealized picture of marriage and family (*AL* 36, 57); he is interested in perceiving the concrete lived reality of marriage and family.

Behind that perspective stands the change from an abstract anthropology, which speaks generally of *the* human being, to a concrete anthropology. It proceeds, as was the case previously, from the fact that all human beings are gifted with understanding and free will and, therefore, have the same dignity. But it takes seriously that we live in time and space as corporeal "incarnated" beings, that we are conditioned by time and space, and that we are on the way in time and space. In each case, we live in a particular time and in a particular culture that has its grandeur, but in comparison with other times and cultures, also has its limits and therefore is, at the same time, subject to change.

This concrete way of looking at things does not exclude but rather includes the fact that there is a basic orientation that is common to all people.[1] In creating human beings as man and woman (Gen 1:27), the Creator has, as it were, written into the heart, and therefore into the conscience, of all human beings such a basic orientation and has given it to them on their journey (Rom 2:14–15). It is referred to as the natural moral law. What is meant are not concrete norms for action, but rather, so to speak, an intuition, an inner compass, an inner voice that urges us to do good and to avoid evil. In connection with a formulation of the International Theological Commission, the pope speaks of an objective source of inspiration for the highly personal process of decision-making (*AL* 305).

In the original sense of the word, even the gospel does not mean a book, much less a codex, in which one can simply look up concrete norms for every individual situation. The gospel, as the law of the new covenant, is, according to Paul, no law carved in stone or written with ink upon parchment; rather, it is a law that is written with the Spirit of the living God in hearts of flesh (2 Cor 3:3). Building on this point, the pope, following Thomas Aquinas, said in his programmatic first apostolic exhortation, *Evangelii gaudium* (2013), that the gospel is "the grace of the Holy Spirit, who is manifested in the faith which works through love" (no. 37).[2]

According to Paul, love is the summary of the entire law (Rom 13:8–10). It is not some vague feeling but rather the fulfillment of the entire law, which goes far beyond the merely legal letter of the law. It fundamentally excludes certain actions, like those that are prohibited in the second tablet of the Ten Commandments,[3] and strongly urges us to take other actions, like those, for instance, that are recommended in the corporal and spiritual works of mercy. In this way, the Word of God is not a kind of travel guide or concrete description of the way, but rather a light for the journey of life (Ps 119:105). It is a light that shines for us like a lantern to the degree that we ourselves are advancing.[4]

This historical understanding is rooted already in Pope John Paul II's apostolic exhortation on marriage and the family, *Familiaris consortio* (1981). In it there is reference to the law of gradualness, that is, the law of steps; however, the pope added that the law of gradualness does not mean gradualness of the law (*FC* 9, 34). The law is always valid and is valid completely, but we can actualize it only incrementally. Pope Francis addresses this distinction many times (*AL* 122, 293–95, 300). He too does not want to change one iota of the law itself. The Word of God concerning sexuality, marriage, and family is valid; it is not to be had at reduced price. It is also not a distant, ultimately unreachable ideal that stands over our life like a polar star a million light-years away. It is a travel companion on the way (*AL* 22).

The goal guides the journey from the first step and determines the direction to be taken; it guides all subsequent steps. However, one can actualize the goal on the way of life only in steps, often only in small steps. Ultimately, we all lag behind the complete realization of the chief commandment of love. For with the commandment to love God with our *whole* heart, with our *whole* soul, and with *all* our mind and to love our neighbor *as* ourselves (Matt 22:37–39) all of us are, to the end of our lives, never finished; with it, we are always only on the way.

MARRIAGE AND FAMILY PASTORAL CARE AS ACCOMPANIMENT

For the pope, the on-the-way character of marriage and family pastoral care results from the on-the-way character of marriage and family. For Pope Francis, pastoral care is accompaniment (*AL* 60, 199–204, 223, 300). He speaks of the divine pedagogy (*AL* 78), of the pedagogy of love (*AL* 211), and of the pedagogy of grace (*AL* 297), which advances often in small steps from one stage to the next (*AL* 122, 273, 295). Pope Francis does not want the pastoral care of the wagging finger, which declares from lofty heights where and how things should be. The method of pastoral care is not the wagging finger, but rather the outstretched hand that is ready to help. In pastoral care, one must do the truth guided by love (Eph 4:15). Pastoral care must accompany people, differentiate situations, and despite all differences, incorporate preferably all and take them along on the way.

For this kind of pastoral accompaniment, mercy in the biblical sense is fundamental. According to the model of the divine pedagogy, it must be the guiding light of all the Church's actions (*AL* 310). Of course, merciful pastoral care is not pastoral care at reduced price or a selling out of the Church's teaching and morality. Rather, it is a matter of pastorally applying a concrete anthropology. Thomas Aquinas already makes that point clear in his commentary on Psalm 42. There he distinguishes the judgment of severity (*severitas*) from the judgment of mercy (*misericordia*). While the former is focused on an abstract picture of the human person, mercy looks at the *conditio personae* and wants to do it justice.[5] It does not impose a general law without distinction but rather seeks to say how this law can be realized in the concrete situation in such a way that it is fair and just.

In this way, mercy does not rescind the general law; rather, it is the higher realization of the law, which sees that justice is done to the concrete, always unique person. One cannot do justice to this uniqueness of every human being with an abstract form of justice, with which the highest justice (*summum ius*) can very quickly become the highest injustice (*summa injuria*). Only that mercy does justice to uniqueness, which does not repeal justice but rather is the higher justice, the excess and the perfection of justice. It alone corresponds to the dignity of each and every unique person. With this position, Pope Francis stands consistently in the tradition and in line with his predecessors.[6]

In this sense, especially the sixth chapter of *Amoris laetitia* speaks of the way of marriage accompaniment. Preparation for marriage begins in the families themselves; they are not only the object but above all the subject of family pastoral care (*AL* 200). There children obtain fundamental impressions for life, also with a view to their own marriage. Families are the original place where one learns about faith and about life in marriage and family. Therefore, *Amoris laetitia* dedicates a separate, extensive chapter to education in the family (*AL* 259–90).

In the parish, the more remote preparation for marriage

begins already in catechesis and in youth ministry. There, it is necessary to disclose the human and Christian meaning of love, the beauty and the happiness of love, sexuality, and marriage—especially today when young people hear so much superficial talk about love, sexuality, and marriage. That cannot happen by simply presenting young people with norms and teaching them an entire catechism; rather, it occurs by imparting, in a concretely tangible and appealing way, the values that are important for marriage and family (*AL* 201, 205, 207). Today, that is truly no easy task, but it is an indispensable and worthwhile task, with which the synod in fall 2018, dedicated to youth, was concerned.

A CATECHUMENATE FOR MARRIAGE?

Amoris laetitia calls the more proximate preparation for marriage "a kind of 'initiation' to the sacrament of matrimony," thus a kind of catechumenate for marriage (*AL* 207; see also *AL* 212–16). When preparation for first communion and for confirmation take weeks or months, and preparation for the sacrament of priestly ordination can in fact take years, it simply cannot be the case that preparation for marriage takes place in only one or two conversations with the pastor, in which they deal primarily with the preparation of the documents and the configuration of the wedding ceremony. In the United States and in different communities in Rome, I have encountered a different experience. In those places, within the context of marriage preparation that extended over multiple group conversations in the evening, they have again introduced in some cases the engagement and an ecclesial engagement celebration. On a number of occasions, at Sunday eucharistic celebrations with the community, I presided over such engagement celebrations, and each time, I—just like the older married people who were present—was deeply moved. In this regard, we in Germany are a developing country when it comes to pastoral care. There is a pressing need to take action.

Even after the wedding, marriage is no finished product. To be sure, with the wedding the marriage is irrevocably concluded and sacramentally confirmed and blessed. Nevertheless, the married couple then become protagonists who "assume an active and creative role in a lifelong project" that they carry forward together (*AL* 218). Accompaniment, therefore, is necessary even after the marriage ceremony. In most marriages and families, crises happen. In such crisis situations, the Church must help; in that process, the first task of the pastor is to contribute to forgiveness and reconciliation (*AL* 41, 105, 242).

The pope also speaks of often-missed opportunities for accompaniment (*AL* 230). One opportunity is the baptism of the first child as well as the first communion of children. In a number of parishes, preparation for first communion is carried out in the form of family catechesis, and it has had good results. For many young parents themselves have little knowledge of what Eucharist means and very often too little experience of the Eucharist. If the parents and the family do not support the communion preparation of children, then it often fizzles out very quickly. In the process of communion preparation, however, young families get to know each other; groups develop and networking takes shape in the community, through which the effort of the first communion instruction is sustained and brings lasting fruit. A new chapter begins when the children become independent and leave the house, and the parents must give new shape to their partnership. Above all, pastoral care for seniors becomes ever more important today in light of the longer life expectancy of most people. Finally, the pastoral care of seniors passes over into end-of-life care—not only of the one who is dying, but also of the broader circle of the family—and, finally, it passes over into grief counseling, when a partner dies and a most difficult, lonely time begins for the other (*AL* 48, 191, 231).

All of that can only be touched on in this context to show how very much *Amoris laetitia* is concerned not with abstract doctrine, but with a concrete understanding and accompaniment of married and family life. Indeed, one would completely misunderstand this concern if one wanted to interpret it as a disoriented, relativistic situational ethics. On the journey of life in marriage and family, in reality, it is a matter of taking the path of actualizing the Christian vision of marriage and family, just as it is attested to in Holy Scripture and in its interpretation in the teaching of the Church. Especially today, with the widespread lack of orientation, that is a fundamental pastoral service that the Church must provide to give a direction and a deeper sense to the life of people by looking toward Jesus.

NOTES

1. In recent times, this question was a much-discussed theme in connection with the encyclical *Humanae vitae* (1968). The pope does not go one more time into the details of this issue; he confines himself to appealing to a document from the International Theological Commission, which deals extensively with the problem of the historicity of the natural moral law and its applicability to concrete situations. Following Thomas Aquinas, it concludes that the natural moral law "cannot supply a norm that can be applied adequately and almost automatically to the concrete situation"; the natural law cannot be understood "as an already established set of rules that impose themselves *a priori* upon the moral subject." Rather, it is "a source of objective inspiration for the deeply personal process of making a decision." See the International Theological Commission, *In Search of a Universal Ethic: A New Look at the Natural Law* (2009), no. 59.

2. With reference to Thomas Aquinas, *Summa Theologiae* I/II, q. 108, art. 1 and q. 30, art. 4.

3. The New Testament knows sins that exclude one from the kingdom of God (1 Cor 6:9–10; Gal 5:19–21), which the Church's tradition acknowledges as so-called absolute norms that are valid everywhere and at all times. See John Paul II's encyclical *Veritatis splendor* (1993), nos. 79–83.

4. See Pope Francis's encyclical *Lumen fidei* (2013).

5. Thomas Aquinas, *Commentary on the Psalms*, 42, lectio 1.

6. See Pope John Paul II's encyclical *Dives in misericordia* (1980), nos. 42, 49; similarly, Pope Benedict in the encyclical *Caritas in veritate* (2009), no. 6, regarding determining the relationship of *caritas* and *iustitia*. Two of the experts who know John Paul II the best, R. Buttiglione and R. Guerra López, have pointed out the continuity between John Paul II and Francis. Concerning this discussion, see Massimo Borghesi, *Jorge Mario Bergoglio: Una biografia intellettuale: Dialettica e mistica* (Milan: Jaca Book, 2017), 254–62. English edition is titled *The Mind of Pope Francis: Jorge Mario Bergoglio's Intellectual Journey*.

Chapter 3

MARRIAGE AND FAMILY UNDER THE BANNER OF GOD'S COVENANT WITH HUMAN BEINGS

Amoris laetitia's understanding of marriage and family is guided by the Second Vatican Council. The council has described and determined that marriage is a community of life and love. In an important statement, the council overcame the authoritative definition, in the old Canon Law of 1917, of marriage as a contract (*contractus*) for the mutual conferral of rights and duties. Instead, the council understood marriage as a covenant (*foedus*) and has thereby integrated it in the larger context of the covenantal history of God with human beings (*AL* 67ff.; see also *GS* 48). With every young couple that promises to make the journey of life together with one other, this history of God with human beings begins anew.

THE CREATIVE REALITY OF MARRIAGE AND FAMILY

The covenantal history of God with human beings begins already with creation (*AL* 9–30). The culmination of the Creation story is the creation of the human being. Nevertheless, as beautiful as it may have been there, Adam as a single person does not feel at all happy in paradise. He lacks an equal partner. Only as God introduces Eve to Adam does he let out a cry of exultation. Finally, that is "flesh of my flesh." He calls Eve *ischa*, literally translated *woman*. That means Eve is his equal companion (Gen 2:23; *AL* 163). Woman is the companion of man; man is the companion of woman. There is no word of the subordination of woman to man in the report of Creation. God has created both man and woman for each other, each created equally in God's image (Gen 1:27). The subordination of woman first occurs because of sin (Gen 3:16). This subordination is established not in the order of creation, but in the order of sin (*AL* 54, 155–56). In the order of redemption, this subordination, according to Paul, has no more validity. For "in Christ" there is neither man nor woman; both are not isolated individuals but rather one (Gal 3:28); the natural differences are not abolished, but they are indeed not momentous when it is a matter of equal personal dignity.[1]

Man and woman receive the mission to be fruitful and to populate the Earth (Gen 1:28). In this way, the future of humanity is entrusted to them. Likewise, in common, man and woman jointly receive a cultural mandate. They should use the goods of the Earth (Gen 1:28–30) and cultivate and care for the Earth (Gen 2:15). The preservation of creation and the configuration of the world is entrusted thereby to them together with the future of humanity.[2]

Marriage and family as the community of life and love of man and woman and of the children who derive from their union are from the primordial beginning of creation, accordingly, *the* primordial human institution, which one cannot simply redefine today. *Amoris laetitia* totally rejects new definitions in ideological forms of gender theory that radically separate biological sex and sociocultural gender and that cede them to our free disposal (*AL* 56).[3] However, besides these ideological forms, there are forms of gender research that must be taken seriously, which ask about the societal and culturally conditioned features of the relationship of man and woman. It is beyond question that there have been and continue to be today such developments in the cultural history of humanity. On the basis of the theme of being on the way, *Amoris laetitia* is open to this; in fact, it really invites serious reflection about it.

A POSITIVE VIEW OF SEXUALITY AND *EROS*

According to the biblical story of Creation, the human being in body and soul is God's good, God's very good, creation. Consequently, in the Creation story, no kind of devaluation of sexuality, *eros*, and marriage can be found. It is only through sin that alienation of the sexes, strife, jealousy, war between the sexes, oppression, infidelity, and lack of chastity come into the world. Many Church fathers, among them also Augustine, saw sexuality and *eros* under this more negative sign. *Amoris laetitia* overcomes this pessimistic view and, in line with Thomas

Aquinas's creation-appropriate view, regards the passions (*passiones*), along with desire, tenderness, and embraces, as something willed and bestowed in creation. That in *Amoris laetitia* now a pope—finally—speaks positively without shame of the erotic dimension of love is nothing less than liberating (*AL* 67, 142–52). Pope Francis quotes the Bible: "Everything created by God is good, and nothing is to be rejected" (1 Tim 4:4; *AL* 61). Every form of Manicheism, every demonization or fundamental suspicion of sexuality and *eros* is thereby clearly rejected.

The passions can be an impetus to good. *Amoris laetitia*, admittedly, also knows that the passions can likewise cause suffering. If they are not cultivated and integrated into the entirety of the person, then they ruin the person and the communal life of marriage and family. For this reason, *Amoris laetitia* speaks very extensively about the task of education, including education concerning sexuality and, above all, the formation of conscience (*AL* 37, 83, 263ff., 280ff., among others). That too is a chapter that one should take very much to heart and ask him- or herself the following: How can we help children and young people achieve a relaxed and simultaneously responsible relation to *eros* and sexuality? Or, have we perhaps opted out of this task for the most part and turned sex education over to other forces?

THE SACRAMENTALITY OF MARRIAGE

The sacrament of marriage takes up the creative dimension of marriage and family, purifies it of the darkening effect and corruption of sin, and perfects it. *Amoris laetitia* unfolds the Christian view in a distinctive way under the heading "Looking to Jesus" (*AL* 58ff.). Again, *Amoris laetitia* is not concerned with abstract norms. Jesus is in person *the* norm of Christian life. He is the measure according to which everything, including sexuality, marriage, and family, takes its bearings.

In the incarnation, Jesus Christ has assumed, redeemed, and sanctified everything that is human, including human love. He purifies it and brings it to perfection. In view of the vulnerability, fragility, and ambiguity of sex and *eros*, which has been caused by sin, the sacrament of marriage has a healing and redeeming function (*gratia sanans*). Beyond that, it sanctifies and perfects the creative reality of marriage (*gratia sanctificans et perficiens*). It bestows on the married couple the ability to bear witness to the love of God in their love and to live out that love (*AL* 67). Therefore, the sacrament of marriage is not a social convention, an empty ritual, or a merely external sign of commitment. It is a reflection of the triune love of God, and following the Letter to the Ephesians in the New Testament, it is an image of the love of Jesus Christ for his bride, the Church (Eph 5:21–32). In this sacrament, the love of Jesus, including his cross and resurrection, becomes sacramentally present. At the same time, the wedding and marriage are preliminary celebrations and foretastes of the heavenly wedding feast (*AL* 71–74).

Every experienced pastor knows that today it is, for the most part, very difficult to open up young couples who sign up for a Church wedding, couples who are of good will but often without sufficient knowledge of the faith, to the entire riches of the Church's teaching about the sacrament of marriage. We may console ourselves with the fact that the Church too needed a long time until it attained clarity finally in the twelfth century about the sacramentality of marriage. We may be confident that the "great mystery" of marriage (Eph 5:32) gradually becomes apparent also to married couples as they undertake their married journey. For this, Thomas Aquinas's statement about implicit faith can be helpful. Following the Letter to the Hebrews 11:6, he declares, "Every Christian must believe that God exists and that he rewards those who seek him." For him, that implies that faith in God, as the ultimate goal and beatitude of human beings, and faith in Jesus Christ, as the way to this goal, embryonically include all the other statements of faith.[4]

One can gradually introduce young people, therefore, to the mystery of the sacrament of marriage. With their church wedding, married couples embark on a common path and place it under God's blessing and promise. Jesus Christ accompanies them and leads them on this way to their happiness. Therefore, by looking to Jesus, they can travel this common path with confidence. In their mutual love and fidelity, the love and the ultimate fidelity of God in Jesus Christ is effectively present in every situation. The blessing and the power of the sacrament accompany them on their entire further path. They go this way not alone; on the basis of the sacrament, the entire Church accompanies them. From such statements and similar embryonic statements, all further statements concerning the great mystery of marriage follow, according to each person's level of individual understanding.

INDISSOLUBILITY AS COMMITMENT

Only in this great, total context is the teaching of the Church concerning the indissolubility of sacramental marriage comprehensible. According to the teaching of the Church, it is grounded in the words of Jesus: "What God has joined together, let no one separate" (Matt 19:6). As such, it belongs to the Church's binding deposit of faith (*depositum fidei*).[5] One must interpret the Lord's words and the teaching of the indissolubility of marriage that is derived from them within the total context of Jesus's message of the coming of the kingdom of God and the message of his mercy.

One may, therefore, not misunderstand Jesus's words as if indissolubility is a yoke imposed on marriage. Talk about the bonds (*vinculum*) of wedlock may not at all be construed in the literal sense of being a chain or manacle. Jesus's words are the promise that God bears the "I do" of the married couple by means of his own yes, that he accompanies the journey of the married couple, heals and transforms hardened hearts, and directs their experience of the way of the cross, which exists in some form in every marriage, toward life in its Easter fullness. Therefore, one must understand the word about the bonds of wedlock as the expression of a gift (*AL* 62). So just as the union of Jesus Christ and the Church is permanent, so too is the union of man and woman in the sacrament of marriage.

The concept of indissolubility expresses this gift character only imperfectly. It derives from contract law, according to which some contracts establish an enduring obligation and are therewith indissoluble. With this juridical concept, man and woman's mutual gift of self, which is sustained by God's covenantal promise, is not adequately expressed. Therefore, *Amoris laetitia* attempts to express the reality that is meant with another, biblically based, and humanly appealing word, namely, with the word *fidelity* (*AL* 77, 123). *Fidelity* is a human and biblical primordial word, which *Amoris laetitia* seizes upon in many places.

The pope thereby succeeds in bringing the Church's teaching to light anew. For in the couple's promise of fidelity, God promises them his fidelity, which sustains fragile, human fidelity, embraces it, strengthens it, and perfects it. God is faithful even when we are unfaithful (2 Tim 2:13). Precisely today, when we live in a culture of the provisional and temporary, indeed living virtually in a throwaway society, the assuring word of God's steadfast fidelity is of great significance also and specifically in the crises and vicissitudes of life (*AL* 39). It is a good message, with which married people can set themselves upright in difficult situations and by which they can orient themselves.

LOVE'S SONG OF PRAISE

For a deeper understanding of the Christian concept of fidelity in love, Pope Francis has propounded, in the fourth chapter of *Amoris laetitia*, a profound and simultaneously very realistic interpretation of the song of praise of love in the thirteenth chapter of Apostle Paul's First Letter to the Corinthians (*AL* 90–125). This is perhaps the most beautiful chapter in the entire exhortation. It is above all suited for marriage preparation as well as for a reflection weekend, retreat, and similar activities for married people.

In this chapter, Paul says of love, "Love is patient; love is kind; love is not envious....It does not insist on its own way; it is not irritable or resentful....It bears all things, believes all things, hopes all things, endures all things. Love never ends" (1 Cor 13:4–8). Those are not romantic-idealistic statements, but rather very realistic and thus very true statements, far beyond every kind of superficial drivel about love.

The statements in this chapter go far beyond purely sentimental romantic love. Romantic love can be something great and beautiful, and it is always impressive when, even after many years, something of that romantic love still remains with older married couples in a quieter and more inward form. But when one overloads the relation of man and woman with expectations of romantic love, then a sense of being overwhelmed by the excessive demands results and leads almost necessarily to disappointment. For every partner is hopelessly overwhelmed, if he or she is supposed to offer the other heaven on earth. No one can do that.

Therefore, human friendship must develop out of purely sentimental love—and that is a very wise word in *Amoris laetitia* (*AL* 123–30). Friendship is also a basic human concept and a basic concept in the Bible. Friendship is not only a matter of feeling; it is trustworthy companionship on the path of life, which rests on the foundation of the same values and interests; it is companionship through thick and thin and on which one can depend in every situation. In this sense, *Amoris laetitia* describes friendship in marriage very realistically as "a mixture of enjoyment and struggles, tensions and repose, pain and relief, satisfactions and longings, annoyances and pleasures" (*AL* 126). It is worthwhile to reflect on this text at length.

THE FRUITFULNESS OF MARRIED LOVE

Romantic love and friendship are great goods. However, man and woman, according to the Bible, are not created only for their small, private happiness. The most valuable thing that exists, human life and the passing on of life, is entrusted to them jointly (Gen 1:28; 2:15). *Amoris laetitia* addresses these questions in the fifth chapter. The exhortation situates itself thereby in the tradition of the council (see *GS* 50–52), the encyclical *Humanae vitae* (1968), and the apostolic exhortation *Familiaris consortio* (1981). But Pope Francis also knows that the question of the fruitfulness of married love is encumbered by various inner-Church conflicts.

Again, Pope Francis succeeds in bringing some of the light of the good news to questions that are debated in the Church. With complete clarity, he highlights the inner connection of married love and the procreation of new life (*AL* 80). A child is not added to married love as something ancillary, so to speak; a child proceeds as the fruit of that love and also contributes to the joy of married love. Therefore, the pope opposes an antibirth mentality and policies that promote contraception (*AL* 42, 222). He encourages the method of family planning that observes the times of natural fertility (*AL* 222). But he remains silent about other methods of family planning, and he avoids every casuistic determination.

In this chapter, one gets the impression that in *Amoris laetitia*, even that which is not said says something. In the next chapter, we will see that this silence about casuistic questions concerning methods of family planning is not an avoidance of the problems, but on the contrary, it confronts the problems. *Amoris laetitia* does this on the basis of a deeper moral-theological reflection on the possibilities as well as the limits of concrete casuistic statements.[6]

That leads the pope to place family planning, as an aspect of the responsible parenthood taught by the Second Vatican

Council (see *GS* 50), in the responsible conscientious decision of the married couple. But he adds one consideration that he regards as important: preservation of the dignity of the partner. Neither partner may pressure the other partner in these matters, and neither may "use" the other for his or her own wishes. In marriage, conversation about all of these questions should lead to an agreement that protects the dignity of the other.

THE FAMILY AS DOMESTIC CHURCH

With children, marriage grows into a family. By family, one ought to understand not only the nuclear family of father, mother, and children. Grandparents, grandchildren, uncles and aunts, nephews and nieces, parents-in-law, sons-in-law and daughters-in-law, often children from a previous marriage, and in a wider sense, not rarely also friends, neighbors, domestic help, and guests also belong to the family. *Amoris laetitia* takes into account this entire web of familial and kin relationships, with its beautiful and happy aspects as well as its often burdensome problems (*AL* 187).

Amoris laetitia, therefore, would like to understand the family above all as a domestic church (*AL* 15, 67, 86–88, 200, etc.). That is an idea grounded in the Bible, but one that unfortunately has fallen very much into oblivion. According to the New Testament, the Church is realized on three levels: as universal Church, as local church, and as domestic church. The domestic church encompassed not only what we today call the nuclear family, but rather the larger family, to which also friends, acquaintances, and guests, among others, belonged. In this sense, "house" in the New Testament is the form of life and, therefore, something like the primordial form that the Church's organization took. The earliest community gathered in their homes (Acts 2:46). For Paul, the network of house churches provided the bases for his missionary activity.

That means marriage and family are not only the object of pastoral care; they themselves are the subjects, the active bearers, of pastoral care. This occurs through the education of children and handing faith on to the children; through praying together in the family, the celebration of the liturgical year (especially during Advent and the Christmas season), the celebration of Christian customs; through missionary activity in their neighborhood and social milieu; through their hospitality and their cooperative, philanthropic, and social engagement (*AL* 186, 324).

In the history of the Church, domestic churches were important above all in situations of persecution. In the Free Churches, especially in Pietism, the concept of domestic church has remained alive. Since the Second Vatican Council, it was again discovered and valued (*LG* 11; *AA* 11).[7] The conciliar statements have fallen on fertile ground in Latin America, Africa, and Asia (e.g., in the Philippines). In many cases, the concept of domestic church became an official pastoral program in the sense of Base Christian Communities or Small Christian Communities.

In view of the situation of the increasing Diaspora and the retreat of the official Church into ever larger mergers of parishes or into huge parishes, the concept of domestic church, even for us, could be a forward-looking option. The less the Church as institution is present in the life-world of people, all the more could domestic churches, in the sense of Small Christian

Communities, be a way that the Church could be present in the world. Christian families and small groups can give convincing witness of the beauty of lived faith simply by their existence in their milieu. Domestic churches could once again become the springboards, the bases, and the epicenters of the new evangelization. In this way, the words cited at the beginning—"The family is the way of the Church"—would be filled with concrete content. Thus, it is true: pastoral priority in the parish and the diocese belongs to the renewed pastoral care of families.

NOTES

1. Naturally, Paul, like the other apostles, is a man of his time, not ours. Consequently, there are also patriarchal statements in the New Testament, the clearest and most well known is the statement that the wife should be subject to her husband in everything (Eph 5:24). Nevertheless, if one studies this and other statements in context more precisely, one can ascertain that Paul, if he does not correct them immediately, balances them with other statements. In the just-mentioned text, this happens with the statement that husbands should love their wives as Christ has loved the Church and has given himself up for it. That idea goes far beyond the recognition of equal status in their partnership. Thus, the New Testament establishes the foundation for what we today call a collaborative understanding; in fact, it goes beyond that. This view could prevail in the Church, as in society generally, only in the course of a long historical process. Today, it must become fully accepted. Anyway, it is striking that women played a prominent role in early Christian communities, far more than in the contemporary society of the time. For us today, that should be a model and incentive to understand the Church not as a latecomer but as a trailblazer.

2. See Pope Francis's encyclical *Laudato si* (2015).

3. The ideological forms of gender theory contradict the Christian understanding of the human person as the unity of body and soul. In essence, it is a matter of anticorporeal, neo-Gnostic theories, which sees the body as a mere instrument that human beings use in a way similar to the way they use a computer, program it, and where necessary, provide it with new software.

4. Thomas Aquinas, *Summa Theologiae*, II/II, q. 1, art. 6, ad 1. Even if Thomas Aquinas's statements about implicit faith are somewhat variable in detail, one can approximately summarize his teaching in these sentences.

5. The indissolubility of marriage was presupposed and taught by the Second Vatican Council as binding Church teaching (*GS* 48).

However, in view of the clauses concerning adultery in Matthew 5:32 and 19:9 and in view of the statements of some Church fathers as well as the praxis of the Eastern Church, the Council of Trent was aware of the problems. In a compromise formulation, it condemned the position of Luther and held firmly the point that the Latin Church's praxis is not wrong; yet, Trent consciously did not condemn but permitted the praxis of the Eastern Church (DH 1807). Thus, a certain latitude remains open in the practical interpretation of the teaching of Trent. The problems that were then left open have since then been conclusively clarified neither theologically and exegetically nor by the magisterium. That does not constitute a break in the teaching of indissolubility as such, but it does leave some leeway for its concrete interpretation. In this context, it must be sufficient for discussion to refer to Hubert Jedin, *Geschichte des Konzils von Trient*, vol. IV/2 (Freiburg i. Br.: Herder, 1975), 96–121; Joseph Ratzinger, *Gesammelte Schriften: Einführung in das Christentum* (Freiburg i. Br.: Herder, 2014), 600–615. Admittedly, one may not use such unsettled questions to obscure what is undoubtedly clear; however, in the theological discussion and in the practical appeal to the teaching of the indissolubility of marriage, one also cannot simply dismiss these questions out of hand.

6. See *EG* 37, with reference to Thomas Aquinas, *Summa Theologiae* I/II, q. 108, art. 1 and q. 30, art 4. In the following chapter, we will need to return to this point once again.

7. In the postconciliar documents, the domestic church has experienced a true resurrection from its deep slumber: Paul VI, *Evangelii nuntiandi* (1975), 58, 71; John Paul II, *Familiaris consortio* (1981), 21; *Redemptoris missio* (1990), 51; *Catechism of the Catholic Church*, 1655–58; Francis, *Lumen fidei* (2013), 52–53. Klaus Krämer and Klaus Vellgut, eds., *Kleine christliche Gemeinschaften: Impulse für eine zukunftsfähige Kirche* (Freiburg i. Br.: Herder, 2012).

CHAPTER 4

SO-CALLED IRREGULAR SITUATIONS

Human beings can fail; Christian marriages and families can also fail. The failure of a marriage and a family is always a human catastrophe. It signifies the failure of a life-project and leads to disappointment; to a feeling of failure; to despondency; often to a radical change in the external lifestyle—living arrangements, the social environment, the circle of friends and acquaintances—and to the necessity to orient oneself in a new way. The ones who suffer are above all the children. For them, the living environment in which they felt snug and secure falls apart. That can lead to the collapse of fundamental human trust, often with traumatic consequences.

MARRIAGES AND FAMILIES IN CRISIS

Pastoral accompaniment is especially necessary in such difficult situations. The pope recalls his famous word about the Church as a field hospital (*AL* 291). But what to do? As pastors, first and foremost, we will advise pardon and reconciliation and do everything we possibly can for that goal. But there are situations in which, after every other reasonable attempt has proven to be in vain, a divorce turns out to be the last resort, something unavoidable, and in many cases, even something morally necessary (*AL* 241–42).

Partners who live alone after divorce deserve support, attention, and a spiritual home in our communities. In most cases, after a divorce a new partnership happens, often a new civil marriage. Pastorally, one will first try to work out the situation in the way that Canon Law has ready at hand, namely, to clarify whether the failed marriage really was a sacramentally valid marriage. Pope Francis has essentially simplified and shortened the canonical procedures that exist for the declaration of matrimonial nullity.[1]

Admittedly, it can be the case that nullity is not able to be proved juridically; however, the marriage partners, perhaps only one of them, are convinced in conscience that the marriage was not valid from the very beginning. It can likewise happen that both or one of them says, "Yes, it was a marriage, we lived well together for years, but then our bond became weaker and finally broke. A way back is excluded because the other does not want it and has already contracted a new union," or, "because I myself have contracted a new civil marriage that is stable and permanent and that I cannot give up without laying new guilt upon myself. For that would be unfaithful to my new partner and would also be irresponsible with regard to our children." What can the Church say about such a situation, and what can it do about it?

THREE CRITERIA FOR MAKING DISTINCTIONS

Amoris laetitia does not give a direct, concrete answer to the question that was posed. Rather, the exhortation says that there is no general, easy recipe (*AL* 298). It is necessary to carefully distinguish situations and, in the process, to do justice to the complexity of the situations (*AL* 296–300). There is a difference between whether someone has actively and intentionally broken and destroyed the marriage or whether he or she was abandoned and forsaken. John Paul II already addressed this difference, admittedly without drawing out its concrete consequences (*FC* 84). *Amoris laetitia* likewise offers no concrete casuistic answer. Instead of getting involved with casuistry, Pope Francis prefers to connect with the spiritual tradition of discerning spirits, of spiritual discernment, which is already established in the Bible and is present through all of the centuries.[2] If one somewhat systematizes the text of the eighth chapter, which is not always entirely clear in its manner of argumentation but is fully clear in its intentions, then three points emerge for the pastoral assessment of the so-called irregular situations.

1. The pope leaves no doubt that civil marriages, de facto partnerships, the unions of the divorced and remarried (*AL* 291), and same-sex partnerships (*AL* 250–51) do not correspond to the Christian understanding of marriage. But he likewise says that some of these partnerships can realize, in a partial and analogous way, elements of a Christian marriage (*AL* 292). Just as elements of the true Church exist

outside of the Catholic Church (see *LG* 15, *UR* 3), so too elements of Christian marriage can be present in the partnerships just mentioned, even when they do not fully realize or do not yet fully realize the ideal. That is true, above all, concerning partnerships characterized by enduring relations, mutual affection and commitment, responsibility and care for one another as well as care and the good upbringing of their children.

Therefore, one ought not to paint the situation in black and white. Even if one cannot equate the so-called irregular situations to a sacramental marriage, nevertheless one ought not to condemn them in a global fashion. One must objectively and fairly appreciate them with regard to what is positive in them and must invite them to take possible steps toward full realization of the ideal (*AL* 292–93; see also 298). People living in such partnerships are not excommunicated; rather, they are invited to participate actively in the life of the Church in the way that is possible in their situation (*AL* 300). *Amoris laetitia* urges us to follow the logic of integration into the community of the Church (*AL* 296).

2. Pope Francis seizes on a second important distinction. He distinguishes between the objective commandment or prohibition and the subjective culpability of the person. That is a traditional distinction, which is also found in the 1993 encyclical from John Paul II, *Veritatis splendor* (nos. 62–64).[3] The distinction means that a weighty subjective peccability does not always, or not always in the same way, correspond to

> the objective gravity of a commandment or prohibition (murder, adultery, serious injury of another, etc.). The Church possesses—as the pope says—a solid body of reflection concerning mitigating factors and circumstances (*AL* 301). He cites the *Catechism of the Catholic Church* and names them: ignorance, inadvertence, duress, fear, habit, inordinate emotional attachments as well as social factors. All of them can mitigate the subjective accountability for an act (no. 1735). This traditional point of view supports once again the concrete anthropological starting point of *Amoris laetitia*, to see and to assess the deeds of a human being in their concrete conditions.[4]

A second point is added. The morality of an act ought not to be seen only under the aspect of the objective norm; it also has a subjective aspect. To count as a serious sin requires not only the violation of an objectively weighty commandment, but also the full understanding of the seriousness of the action and the intention to violate God's commandment. This subjective responsibility is not the same in all cases (*AL* 79). The weakness of many criticisms of *Amoris laetitia* is that they represent a one-sided moral objectivism and do not consider the subjective dimension, which is an essential element of moral action.

According to *Amoris laetitia*, nevertheless, in judging an action, one must consider the state of the person's conscience and ask, Has the person in question really recognized, or could they have recognized, the act as bad and has the person freely willed it as contrary to God's will? The individual's conscience is decisive (*AL* 303). To the extent that a human being in conscience recognizes personal guilt, he or she obviously must be sorry for the fault and embark on the path of conversion (*AL* 297, 300). He or she is not permitted to flaunt what is objective sin or to willfully present it as if it is the Christian ideal (*AL* 297). The Church must help to form consciences and must, in the process, present the objective norm, but it cannot put itself in the place of conscience (*AL* 37). Emphasis on the dignity of individual conscience is one of the strongest points in the thought and proclamation of Pope Francis; with this emphasis, he stands completely on the ground of Vatican II, which characterized conscience as the most secret core and sanctuary of human beings (*GS* 16).

The distinction between the objective and the subjective dimension is important for the interpretation of canon 915 in Canon Law, the only canon in the current Canon Law that is relevant for our question. The canon says that if someone stubbornly persists in serious sin, then he or she cannot be given absolution and be admitted to communion. This canon is absolutely sensible; one can only approve of it fully and completely. In the internal forum, it is a matter of clarifying whether, in the concrete situation, de facto subjectively serious culpability and stubbornness are present, so that that which is valid *de iure* must be applied. If, after conscientious examination, this is not the case, then in the internal forum, if nothing else is in the way, absolution and therewith admission to communion is possible. If the danger exists that public scandal might arise as a result, it is a matter of pastoral prudence to advise the penitent to go to communion in a different community or at a pilgrimage site.[5]

3. The final distinction, following Thomas Aquinas, concerns the distinction between a general law and its concrete application. All general laws are imperfect

> because they do not foresee all concrete circumstances, and, therefore, they also cannot concretely govern in advance all situations. When it is a matter of conduct (practical reason), one cannot, in a purely deductive and logically compelling way, derive the concrete application from a general law, especially in complex situations; this is different from the procedure of speculative reason. According to the teaching of Thomas Aquinas, concrete application happens in the realm of practical reason with the help of the cardinal virtue of prudence, which is guided by love and mercy. It is, so to speak, the situational conscience.[6] The more concrete and more specific the application becomes, so much more uncertain it becomes and a fortiori errors creep in.[7]

That is not to be understood in the sense of situation ethics, which acknowledges no general laws. Prudence respects the law; it does not invalidate the law; it also does not change the law or even make an exception. Rather, prudence decides *how* the law is to be so applied in a concrete situation that it is just and fair, and it does this guided by love and mercy (*AL* 304–5).[8]

Therefore, there can be no general recipe (*AL* 298), especially in complex situations, and there can be no casuistic, statutory rules that can be applied to every individual case (*AL* 300). In the particular case, one must arrive at a prudent application of the general norm, guided by mercy (*AL* 309–11). Above all, in light of mercy, one is not permitted to condemn or exclude anyone forever (*AL* 296–97). On the contrary, mercy requires, after a period of reflection and contrition, that an opportunity for a new beginning is kept open for everyone.[9]

WHAT IS IN EFFECT NOW?

After the presentation of these three points, we can ask in conclusion the following: What do these three points mean for dealing pastorally with the so-called irregular situations, especially the thorny issue of admitting divorced and remarried individuals to communion? As has been said already, *Amoris laetitia* does not give an explicit answer to this question. The pope has clearly said that the magisterium does not always have to decide everything (*AL* 3), and he does not want to set up a concrete rule, which only leads once again to a new casuistry (*AL* 304). Therefore, it was entirely consistent that he, in fact, put forth principles whose concrete application in the concrete situation, however, was left to spiritual discernment.

In this context, contested note 351 is intelligible, which says that in certain cases, participation in the sacraments can be helpful (*AL* 305). The uproar that resulted concerning this explanatory note is difficult to comprehend, in view of the decree of the Council of Trent concerning the Eucharist. For the Council of Trent expressly declared that the Eucharist is an antidote that frees from daily sins and preserves from mortal sins (DH 1638).[10] The corresponding canon further strengthens this statement and emphasizes that the fruit of the Eucharist is the remission of sins, whereby a restriction to venial sins is not mentioned (DH 1655). Who wants, therefore, to dispute the fact that reception of the sacrament of the Eucharist can be recommended in certain so-called irregular situations?

If one reads note 351 on the foundation provided by the Council of Trent and in the context of the entire exhortation, then it can only mean that, on account of the mentioned principles and their observance, there *can* be a pastorally responsible, merciful decision in favor of admission to the sacraments in *certain*, that is, not in *all*, situations, after an appropriate period of spiritual reflection and examination.

A series of statements from Pope Francis in the aftermath of *Amoris laetitia* point in this direction, such as his letter to the Argentine bishops of the Buenos Aires region (September 5, 2016) and his statement on his return flight from Lesbos (September 16, 2016).[11] Some individual bishops and bishop conferences have also interpreted *Amoris laetitia* in this way. That is the interpretation that I endorse and that I am convinced is possible—in fact, is commanded—on the basis of the Church's tradition.[12]

After the pope has rightly established that he cannot give a concrete answer for the universal Church because situations around the world are too different, it appears to me that now the task and the sacred obligation of bishops and of the higher religious superiors is, on the foundation of *Amoris laetitia*, and in conversation with priests and coworkers who are charged with providing marriage and family pastoral care, to work out criteria that are tailored to the respective concrete situation. The Council of Trent as well as the authoritative canon of current Canon Law open free spaces, in which responsible pastoral decisions can be made and also must be made for the health and salvation of affected individuals.

A PARADIGM SHIFT?

In *Amoris laetitia*, Pope Francis lays out points for judging the issue of admitting divorced and remarried people to communion in certain, individual situations. He opens the door and shows a possible path, but he does not walk through the door or develop canonical rules applicable for all concrete situations. He does this, not out of weakness, but conscious that no universally valid, concrete implications for action can be derived from general principles. That is not situation ethics, which recognizes no universally valid norms. According to Catholic teaching, the general law is valid always and in every case; but there are constitutive, subjective essential conditions of the moral act and circumstances, which can mitigate the level of subjective responsibility. Therefore, one may not casuistically and rigorously overextend the concrete possibilities of applying the natural moral law or the gospel to complex, concrete situations. Virtue resides in the middle between laxity and rigorism.[13]

One can understand the position of *Amoris laetitia* only if one understands that it turns away from an abstract anthropology and adopts a concrete anthropology, which proceeds not generally from *the* human being but rather from human beings in their concrete external and internal situation and which respects them in their always unique dignity. One cannot do justice to the uniqueness of each human being with an abstract form of justice. Only mercy will do justice to the uniqueness of each human being and his or her situation. It does not rescind justice; rather, it is the higher righteousness, the abundance and perfection of justice. It alone corresponds to the dignity of every unique person. With this position, Pope Francis—as has been shown—stands consistently in the tradition, especially in the tradition of Thomas Aquinas and in line with his predecessors.[14]

Some have characterized the position of *Amoris laetitia* as a turning point in moral theology and as a perspective and paradigm shift.[15] I would not like to speak of a turning point because nothing is being changed regarding objective norms. However, one can speak of a shift in perspective and paradigm, provided that one understands both terms correctly. Correctly understood, a paradigm shift changes nothing in the existing laws; rather, it places the laws in a more comprehensive, new, or—in this case in the original biblical and Thomistic—horizon and mercifully applies them, in the horizon of the biblical message, so that they can do justice to the concrete living situation and to the concrete way of life of a concrete human being and can accompany him or her with counsel and help as he or she takes further steps on his or her life's path. It is a matter not of *innovation* but of *renewal* on the basis of a return to the original Thomistic tradition, which has not been narrowed in a neo-Thomistic way.

One can call this a paradigm shift because this renewal pertains not only to a concrete, delimited problem, but to moral theology generally and, therefore, has ramifications for many similar situations. Obviously, that does not mean that with *Amoris laetitia* all of these problems have already been solved in one fell swoop. The vision of *Amoris laetitia* is, rather, a challenge for further theological reflection and for pastoral praxis to think more along the lines shown by the apostolic exhortation and to think anew through the pending, pressing problems. *Amoris laetitia* points explicitly to this fundamental challenge in the final chapter.

NOTES

1. Pope Francis, motu proprio *Mitis iudex Dominus Jesus* (2015) and motu proprio *Mitis et misericors Jesus* (2015).

2. In the New Testament, discernment of spirits is a special spiritual charism (1 Cor 12:10; 1 Thess 5:19–21; 1 John 4:1). It plays a significant role already in the desert fathers, the Church fathers, monastic spirituality, and, later, mysticism. According to the Rule of Benedict of Nursia, the abbot is supposed to govern everything temperately with *discretio* as the mother of the virtues (64, 70). The discernment of spirits was fundamental then above all in the spirituality of the Exercises of Ignatius of Loyola, out of which tradition Pope Francis comes. The art of deliberative discernment is found, moreover, in the traditional guidelines for confessors. Only in more recent times has it fallen all too much into oblivion. Pope Francis has now lifted this old tradition into the light anew.

3. Cf. Thomas Aquinas, *Summa theologiae*, I/II, q. 19, art. 15: "Therefore, the act of willing will be bad, since it wills something bad; not, to be sure, something that is bad *per se*, but something that is bad *per accidens* because of reason's apprehension." (*Unde voluntas erit mala, quia vult malum: non quidem id, quod est malum per se, sed id, quod est malum per accidens, propter apprehensionem rationis.*)

4. See *EG* 37, with reference to Thomas Aquinas, *Summa Theologiae* I/II, q. 108, art. 1 and q. 30, art 4; and Thomas Aquinas, *Commentary on the Psalms*, 42, lectio 1.

5. Concerning the canonical aspect of this issue, see Cardinal Francesco Coccopalmerio (who is responsible for legislative texts), *A Commentary on Chapter Eight of Amoris Laetitia* (New York: Paulist Press, 2017).

6. See Thomas Aquinas, *Summa theologiae* II/II, q. 47, art. 1 and 2 about the virtue of prudence as the proper rational provision in the realm of conduct. See also note 4 above.

7. *Summa theologiae*, I/II, q. 94, art. 4, cited in *AL* 304.

8. This hermeneutic of application was described by Gadamer, following Aristotle, on whom Thomas draws. Hans Georg Gadamer, *Truth and Method* (New York: Continuum, 1975), 274–305.

9. One can ask whether, with other words and in a new form, the practice of some church leaders, which is attested to by Origen (Commentary on Matthew 14, 23) and which so important a Church father as Basil of Caesarea made his own (Epistle 217, 77), is taken up, namely, allowing leniency and mercy to prevail for Christians who live in a second marriage so that, after a period of penance, they are admitted again to full ecclesial community. Because this question is not taken up in *Amoris laetitia*, we can ignore it in this context.

10. Concerning this question, see Thomas Aquinas, *Summa theologiae* III, q. 79, art. 3f. and 6. According to him, the one who is conscious (!) of being in a state of serious sin and remains attached to this sin (!) is excluded from reception of the Eucharist. For Thomas too, the subjective situation of conscience is therefore decisive. Venial sins, however, are forgiven through the eucharistic sacrament. In this case, the sacrament is a help in order to make progress on the path of salvation. Imperfect contrition is sufficient for reception because it is perfected through the grace of the sacrament.

11. After the completion of the manuscript by Pope Francis, this interpretation was expounded as the officially valid exegesis of *Amoris laetitia*.

12. Others see therein a break with the traditional discipline, according to which divorced and remarried individuals can be admitted to communion only when they promise to live together celibately (*FC* 84). Apart from the question whether this tradition really and historically is as general as is claimed (cf. Thomas Aquinas, *Summa Theologiae*, II/II, q. 1, art. 6, ad 1; and note 9 above), the mentioned condition is not a doctrine, and definitely not a dogma, but an ecclesial (!) discipline, which has been derived from the doctrine of the indissolubility of marriage. It must be interpreted and applied like every discipline according to the generally recognized theological and canonical rules that are likewise found in the tradition. Simply

to collect historical testimonies of this discipline and to impose them indiscriminately on every situation, without the theological and juridical hermeneutic of application that is demanded by the tradition, is a juridical and theological positivism, which contradicts the gospel as well as every halfway thought-out jurisprudence. In this matter, the apostolic exhortation *Amoris laetitia* does nothing other than to recall anew important pastoral possibilities of these traditional rules. In doing this, the exhortation stands entirely on the ground of ecclesial tradition.

13. That is true for all virtues, according to Thomas. See *Summa theologiae* I/II, q. 64, art. 6.

14. See note 4 above.

15. Stephan Goertz and Caroline Wittig, *Amoris laetitia: Wendepunkt für die Moraltheologie?* (Freiburg im Breisgau: Herder, 2016). In a similar direction: Walter Kasper, "*Amoris laetitia*: Bruch oder Aufbruch. Eine Nachlese," *Stimmen der Zeit* 141 (2016): 723–32; Eberhard Schockenhoff, "Traditionsbruch oder notwendige Weiterbildung? Zwei Lesearten des nachsynodalen Schreibens *Amoris laetitia*," *Stimmen der Zeit* 142 (2017): 147–58; Paul M. Zulehner, *Vom Gesetz zum Gesicht: Ein neuer Ton in der Kirche. Papst Franziskus zu Ehe und Familie* (Ostfildern: Patmos, 2016).

Chapter 5

THE SPIRITUALITY OF THE *MAGIS* IN MARRIAGE AND FAMILY

Amoris laetitia concludes not with the chapter on the so-called irregular situations but with a chapter on spirituality in marriage and family. That shows once again what is decisively important to the apostolic exhortation. It does not concern canonical rules, which are without a doubt necessary in their proper realm and which can also be salutary; rather, it concerns spiritual discernment, accompaniment, encouragement, inspiration, and integration.

In this sense, the pope summarizes once again what is most important: marriage and family as a path, ultimately as a path of sanctification on which the Holy Spirit constantly urges individuals to go further and transcend the boundaries of what has already been achieved, the family as the place where the love of the triune God indwells. The final section reads, "All of us are called to keep striving towards something greater than ourselves and our families, and every family must feel this constant impulse. Let us make this journey as families, let us keep walking together. What we have been promised is greater than we can imagine. May we never lose heart because of our limitations, or ever stop seeking that fullness of love and communion which God holds out before us" (*AL* 325).

That is not the wide path of accommodation to the situation; it is not the path of a cheap—or misunderstood liberal—laissez-faire; and it also is not the comfortable path of easily managed recipes and prescriptions. It is the essentially more difficult, steep path of love, which surpasses everything and conquers everything, which, with always new incitements, is not pulled down but rather follows the urging of the Spirit of God, which lifts us toward the heavens. In these words, we see that the spirit of the Jesuit Jorge Mario Bergoglio is drawn from the school of Ignatius of Loyola. In his Exercises, the idea of the *magis*, the "always more" and the "always better," plays a decisive role.[1]

This "always more" describes the high route of Christian freedom expressed in ever greater love, to which Pope Francis would like to lead us. He goes far beyond all fundamentally comfortable, purely casuistic thinking and acting. By listening to one's personal conscience on the path of spiritual discernment, the way of the *magis* leads to letting oneself be challenged again and again by God's Holy Spirit and being conformed in ever more and better ways to God's call. That is not a conservative position in the false sense, which lets everything remain unchanged, but it also is not a liberal position; rather, it is, in the good sense of the word, a radical position, that is, one that goes to the root (*radix*) and takes the challenge of the gospel seriously.

Unfortunately, we have forgotten and have unlearned to a great extent the art or, better said, the charism of spiritual discernment. Pastors and married couples must get familiar with it anew, cherish it anew, practice it anew, and—above all—petition God for it in prayer. As it appears to me, that is the genuine and truly future-oriented challenge that *Amoris laetitia* presents to us. Therefore, we should not let a narrow, inflexible discussion of a single sentence in a footnote, which one can correctly understand if of goodwill, spoil our joy at the many good statements of *Amoris laetitia*. Rather, we should gratefully seize the challenge that the apostolic exhortation contains and understand *Amoris laetitia* as a *Kairos* moment in order to let the era of mercy, which Pope Francis has introduced by advancing the work of his predecessors, become an era of new joy (*laetitia*) in the Church rather than an era of deplorable conflicts.

NOTE

1. That is expressed first in the Foundation of the Exercises, then again in the meditation on the two standards and in the reflection on the three classes of people as well as on the three kinds of humility.

ABOUT THE AUTHOR

Walter Cardinal Kasper, born 1933; Dr. theol., Professor of Dogmatics; 1989–1999, Bishop of the Diocese of Rottenburg–Stuttgart; 2001, elevated to Cardinal; President of the Pontifical Council for the Promotion of Christian Unity and the Commission for Religious Relations with the Jews as well as member of the Congregation for the Doctrine of the Faith and of the Congregation for the Oriental Churches.

Walter Cardinal Kasper is the main author of the first volume of the *Katholischer Erwachsenenkatechismus* and the editor-in-chief of the third edition of the *Lexikon für Theologie und Kirche*. His numerous theological publications include the following: *The God of Jesus Christ*; *Jesus the Christ*; *An Introduction to Christian Faith*; *Theology and Church*; *The Catholic Church: Nature, Reality, and Mission*; *Wege zur Einheit der Christen: Schriften zur Ökumene I*; *Einheit in Jesus Christus: Schriften zur Ökumene II*. His collected works are being published by Herder Publishing in Freiburg-im-Breisgau, Germany.

At his first Angelus address, Pope Francis praised Kasper's book *Mercy: The Essence of the Gospel and the Key to Christian Life* (Paulist Press, 2014). An aid to understanding Pope Francis's pontificate was published in 2015: *Pope Francis' Revolution of Tenderness and Love: Theological Roots and Pastoral Perspectives* (Paulist Press, 2015).